THE HIDDEN GREEN MAN IN ESSEX

Susan Hegedus

COUNTRY BOOKS

Published by Country Books/Ashridge Press
Courtyard Cottage, Little Longstone, Bakewell,
Derbyshire DE45 1NN

Tel: 01629 640670
e-mail: dickrichardson@country-books.co.uk
www.countrybooks.biz

ISBN 978-1-906789-60-2

British Library Cataloguing in Publication Data.
A catalogue record for this book is available from the British Library.

Printed and bound in England by 4edge Ltd, Hockley, Essex

DEDICATION

In memory of my parents
Margaret Stanley 1923 -1988 and Arthur Stanley 1925 - 2004

For Anthony, Amy, Sam and Oliver with love

Acknowledgements

With grateful thanks to Ruth Wylie – Green Man enthusiast extraordinaire who has given me so much help. Special thanks to Clara McDermott, Deirdre McBurney, Kristin De Freitas and Susan Anderson who have always encouraged me to write and Anthony, my husband who would drive off at a moment's notice to some far-flung church to take photos of this elusive character.

Biography

Susan Hegedus enjoys exploring medieval churches. A large number of them are found in nearby villages where she lives in Essex, England. She plays traditional Irish music on the flute and banjo and has a keen interest in local history. www.susanhegedus.com

The medieval churches of Essex house one of history's best kept secrets. They are frequently inhabited by a mysterious carving of an ancient male head, with foliage, usually oak leaves emerging from his mouth, ears, nose or eyes. He is surprisingly common in Essex, has many guises and is concealed in nooks, roofs, sometimes barely discernible on fonts, but may also be found lurking on roofs, walls, and hidden niches of churches.

However in 1939, folklorist Lady Raglan brought this imagery to public attention by giving this inexplicable bodiless effigy a name. She coined the term "Green Man" in an article for the *Folklore Journal*. Up until then the Green Man had been dismissed by historians and architects as "leaf foliage" or "grotesque face".

But how did the Green Man find his way into churches? It was evident that the only way the Church would achieve any measure of success was to incorporate earlier religions by building churches on pagan sacred sites. The Cross on which Christ was crucified has been referred to as a "Sacred Tree" and became a universal symbol of Christianity.

Leaf masks appeared in Roman art during the 1st century AD and also decorated tombs, many belonging to wealthy wine merchants. These earliest designs had the familiar mournful expression and staring eyes of their future medieval descendants. But the earliest example of a Green Man in a church is in Trier Cathedral, Germany. It was brought from a Roman temple built into a pillar. [Figure 1]

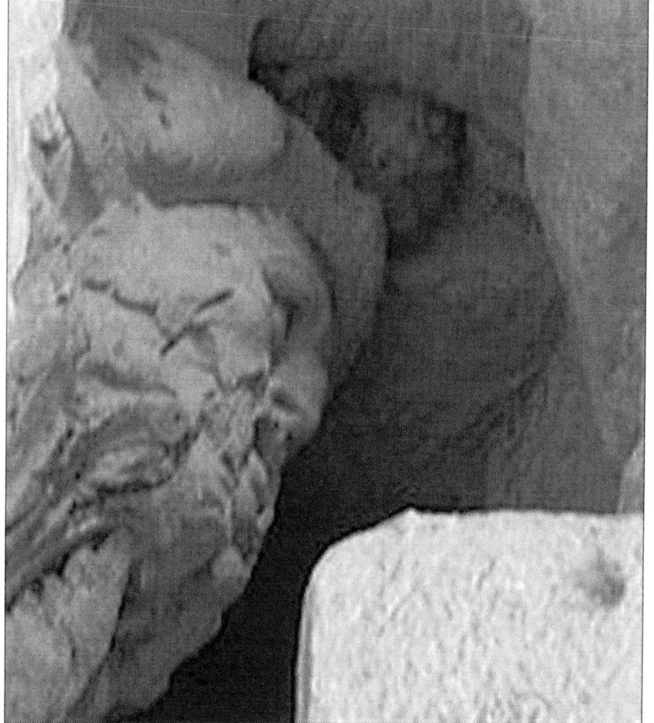

Figure 1: *Triers Cathedral, Germany*

FIGURE 2: *Poitiers Cathedral, France*

Green Men began to appear on Christian tombs; there is a 5th century one at Poitiers, France. Branches of foliage come from the nostrils resembling a huge moustache. [FIGURE 2]

He may be a forerunner to early English 13th century Green Men who similarly emit symmetrical branches from the mouth or nostrils. One such Green Man is found in St Giles' Church, Mountnessing. He stares out from a capital on the north aisle. Branches come from his mouth, making him look as though he has a moustache. [FIGURE 3]

Similarly St Mary the Virgin Church in Widdington, has a 13th century Green Man appearing next to a window in the chancel. His horrific bulbous head also looks moustached. He appears to resemble some kind of octopus or sea urchin and his foliage resembles fronds of seaweed. [FIGURE 4]

In the 12th century, instead of an image of a human face there were sometimes Green Cats but they disappeared, as carvings acquired more distinctive personalities.

There is a fantastic example of one such carving in St Nicholas' Church, Castle Hedingham. An upside down cat appears on the stoup. He is adorable and important for being one of the few 12th century examples in Essex. [FIGURE 5]

FIGURE 4: *St Nicholas' Church, Castle Hedingham*

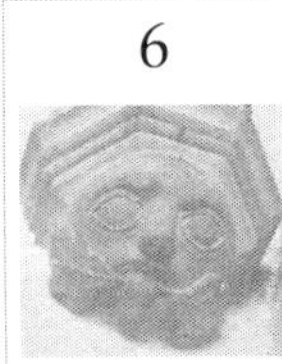

Figure 3: St Giles' Church, Mountnessing

FIGURE 4: *St Mary the Virgin Church, Widdington*

Another early 13th century Green Man overlooks the congregation of the church of St Peter ad Vincula in Coggeshall. This intriguing wooden roof boss has leaves rising up from his forehead with ringlets of foliage shaping the face. The figure-of-eight mouth is a telltale sign of an early 13th century Green Man and is extremely rare. [Figure 6]

The Green Man was first introduced into England after the Norman Conquest and although pagan in origin, became part of the symbolic language of the Church. In the 14th and 15th centuries the Green Man became incredibly popular and many new ones appeared.

As the Black Death raged through England in the 14th century almost half the population died. Consequently labour was more sought after and the working man became valued and was left not only with a new awareness of his worth but also a greater say in his terms of employment. In particular, the prosperity of the Essex wool trade allowed the affluent to build, enlarge and redesign their parish churches, so masons became very sought after.

Old forest gods such as Silvanus, a Roman god representing the fertility cycle of growth, flowering and decay, became set in stone by imaginative masons. Silvanus fell in love with Cyparissus and so turned her into a cypress tree. Consequently he is sometimes represented carrying a branch of a tree. Similar legends also exist in the Middle East and India. The Egyptian green-skinned god Osiris is an example. He was entombed inside a tree by his twin brother Seth and only resurrected by the loving devotion of his wife Isis.

Yet Silvanus was in fact never represented as a leaf mask in Roman art. It seems that masons therefore manipulated the Green Man to compliment their own fantasies and personal interpretations. Subsequently a new freedom of interpretation spread amongst masons, who also became open to a creative continental influence. It is not unusual to see the Green Man depicted as numerous Greco-Roman vegetation Gods and aspects of him are found in Virbius, Pan, Bacchus, Adonis and Silvanus.

The Green Man featured on the font at St Andrew's in Bulmer is one such example. The mason appears to have chosen him to represent Bacchus, the god of wine – a prominent Green Man, luscious with vines and grapes coming from his mouth and forehead. Unusually, St Andrew's had a photo of the Green Man covering the back of a church pamphlet. It is described

Figure 6: *St Peter ad Vincula Church, Coggeshall*

as: *In the nave is the C.15 baptismal font – perhaps the finest of its date in the county. It has shields or angels holding shields around the bowl, and one panel that shows a pagan fertility symbol that appeared in Christian churches throughout the medieval period and gave its name to many pubs – the Green Man.* [FIGURE 7]

Another prominent but unexpected late 15th century Green Man comes in the form of an ornate beautifully carved wooden poppyhead in the church of St Andrew in the village of Belchamp St Paul. A booklet at this church described the two misericords as *grotesque and foliated*, and they certainly are, but one of them is a Green Man. However there is no mention of this, possibly because the Green Man can be elusive, while staring straight at him you may not immediately spy his face. This particular Green Man can be agreeable and sinister at the same time. [FIGURE 8]

Many a Green Man can appear hidden, as is the case of the Green Man outside on the west wall of the 13th century church, St Mary the Virgin Church in Kelvedon. He is smothered by a mass of oak leaves. One has to look quite closely to make out any face at all. The date is questionable as he has been significantly restored in the Victorian era. This is apparent as the leaves seem too crisp to be purely medieval. [FIGURE 9]

A 15th century stone carving is concealed on the right hand side of the South Porch at St Mary's Church in Great Canfield. A single oak leaf stems from each side of his chin. What really struck me was how easy it would be to miss this Green Man, as on the left hand side a similar face appears, but instead of carved oak leaves there are peacocks. [FIGURE 10]

At St Mary the Virgin Church in Sheering, on the outside of the church is a frieze panel with a cramped head hiding beneath a leaf. This Green Man would be so easy to overlook, as without closer inspection he appears merely as decorative foliage. [FIGURE 11]

This 13th century Green Man is situated above the South Doorway of St Augustine's Church in the village of Birdbrook. It is cleverly "hidden". But if you look carefully you will see the face and the foliage which seems to stem from the eyes and sweep round the mouth. [FIGURE 12]

The 11th century *Holy Cross and St Lawrence Church* in Waltham Abbey (known as the Abbey) has a Green Man which appears at the top of a capital concealed on the west doorway, high above you. He could easily be

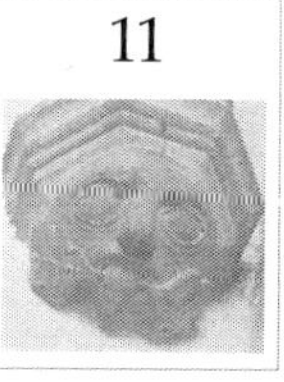

Figure 7: *St Andrew's Church, Bulmer*

Figure 8: *Belchamp St Paul*

FIGURE 9: *St Mary the Virgin Church in Kelvedon*

FIGURE 10: *St Mary's Church, Great Canfield*

Figure 11: *St Mary the Virgin Church, Sheering*

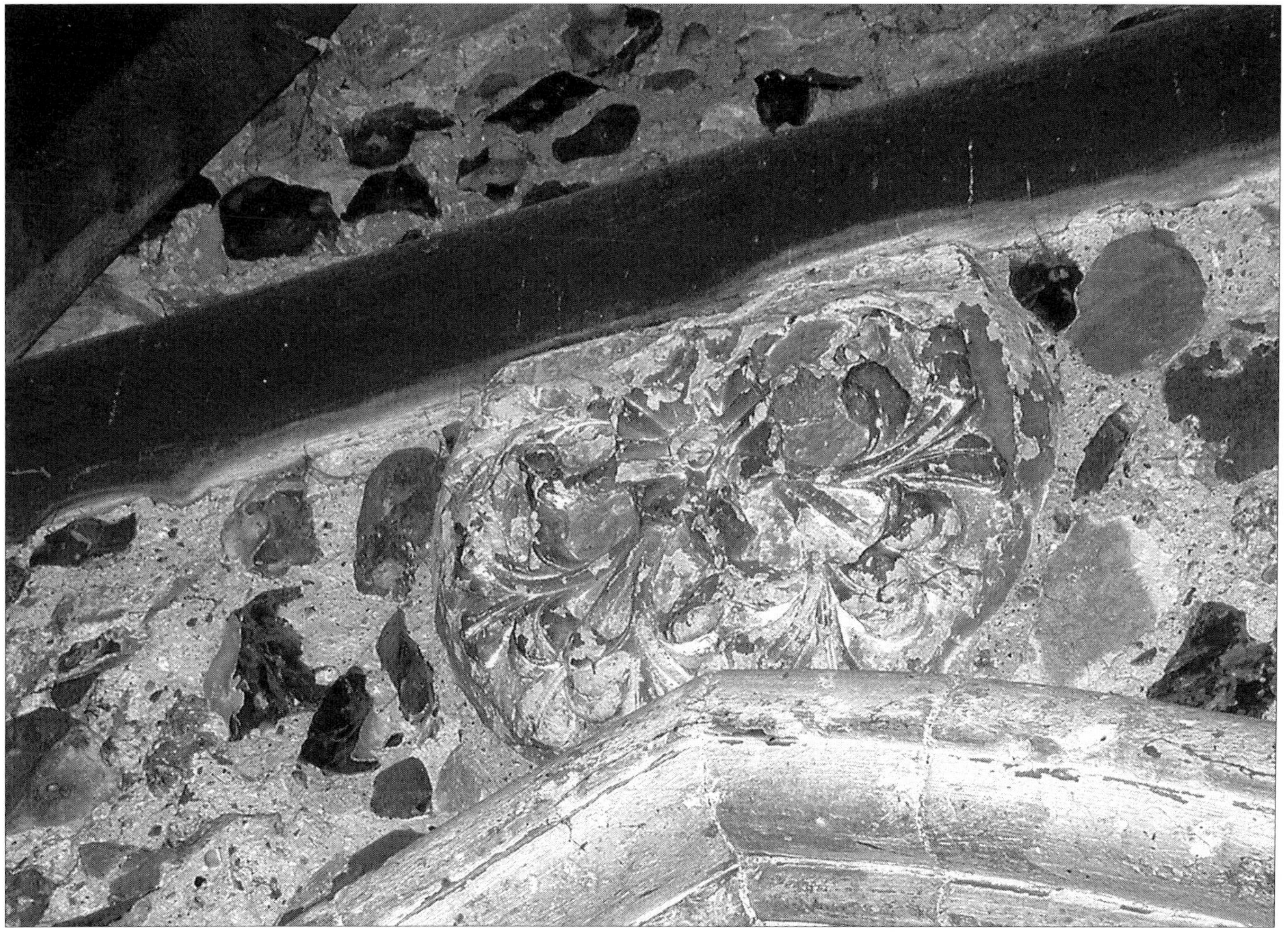

FIGURE 12: *St Augustine's Church, Birdbrook*

mistaken for a leafy decoration as his head is entwined in foliage. This 14th century Green Man is generally thought to represent the Celtic deity, Cernunnos, who was paired with the Roman god deity Mercury. However he is also known as Lord of the Hunt and is associated with the stag, a particularly hunted beast. This church used to look out on to hunting fields, and perhaps that is where the mason acquired his inspiration. [Figure 13]

According to folklore, the Lord of the Hunt was married to Godda, Queen of the Fairies. There are many places in England connected with Godda, Good Easter in Essex being one of them. It used to be called *Godithestre*, or *Godda's sheepfold*.

St Mary the Virgin Church in Matching houses a Green Man with a god-like stature. He is a corbel on the south wall above a window. A single small oak leaf comes from each side of the mouth. The carving appears to have been reset in a modern square neck and painted over, so it is difficult to determine its date; it may be 14th century. [Figure 14]

At All Saints Church in Maldon there is a 14th century Green Man on a capital near the South door. A leaf emerges from the right hand side of his mouth. The left side is damaged, so the leaf on the other side is now detached, but would have been joined by a stem to the left side of his mouth. [Figure 15]

St Mary the Virgin Church in Shenfield dates back to the 13th century but was practically rebuilt in the 15th century. If you enter through the south door and turn left into the tower you will find a 15th century elfin faced Green Man on the front panel of a font. In the 19th century a minister insisted on replacing it with a very expensive Italian marble font and the original was thrown into the rectory garden for a hundred years. In the early 1930s, the ancient font once again entered the church and has been there ever since and so the Green Man takes his rightful place once more. [Figure 16]

All Saints Church in Great Oakley has two late 15th century Green Men appearing on a panel over a doorway that was bricked up years ago. One is bashed but foliage is still discernible, emerging from his mouth and curling up around the sides of his face. [Figures 17 & 18]

St Mary and St Edward Church in West Hanningfield dates back to the 12th century and houses two Green Men. If you enter through the south door, a

Figure 13: *Waltham Abbey*

FIGURE 14: *St Mary the Virgin Church, Matching*

Figure 15: *All Saints Church, Maldon*

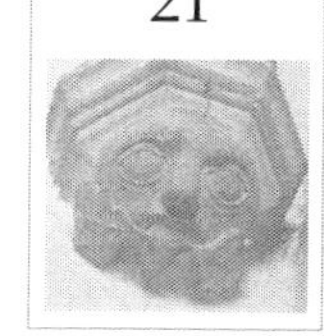

Figure 16: *St Mary the Virgin Church, Shenfield*

Figures 17 & 18: *All Saints Church, Great Oakley*

14th century font is immediately on your left. A tiny Green Man is carved, along with other faces on the panels. One has to look quite closely to make out the face and foliage coming from his mouth. [FIGURE 19]

In contrast, the belfry at the west end of the church has narrow steps leading you up to a late 15th century Green Man with a plump face subtly wreathed with thin leaves. It is enthralling that you can actually touch this wooden carving rather than viewing it from a distance. [FIGURE 20]

All Saints Church in Great Braxted dates back to the 11th century. As you enter through the south porch, immediately on your right is a beautifully gentle and expressive 15th century Green Man with oak leaves spreading out from his face. On closer inspection however, you will notice the veins and outlines of leaves have been recently drawn. [FIGURE 21]

St Martin's 11th century church in Colchester has a conservation order and a large padlock on the outside door when I last visited there. But this did not deter me from experiencing a remarkable 15th century wooden Green Man with foliage sprouting from his ears and around the entire head. He plays the role of roof boss and is perched on a tie beam over what would have been the chancel. A key is available from the Castle Museum nearby. [FIGURE 22]

Other types of imagery residing inside churches are loaded with meaning. St Michael's Church in Great Sampford is particularly rich in animal imagery and houses a *Chimera*, a Greek word meaning a fire-breathing she-monster made up of a lion's head, a goat's body and a serpent's tail – this particular chimera includes a monkey and an owl. In the medieval period it was a common word used to describe a decorative cluster of animals. Today it's used increasingly in Catholic circles to describe the human-animal hybrid embryos conceived in laboratories. The medieval meaning was two-fold. It acted as a warning against lustful appetites and represented the devil in disguise.

The monkey and owl in particular were thought to symbolise evil. If you look carefully at this photo in St Michael's Church in Great Sampford, the cluster also includes a tongue-poking lion-mask, and a green pig. [FIGURE 24]

Pig imagery in churches is peculiar to Essex. Pigs were particularly associated with fertility. Their plump shape was thought to represent pregnancy and abundance.

FIGURE 19: *St Mary and St Edward Church, West Hanningfield*

Figure 20: *St Mary and St Edward Church, West Hanningfield*

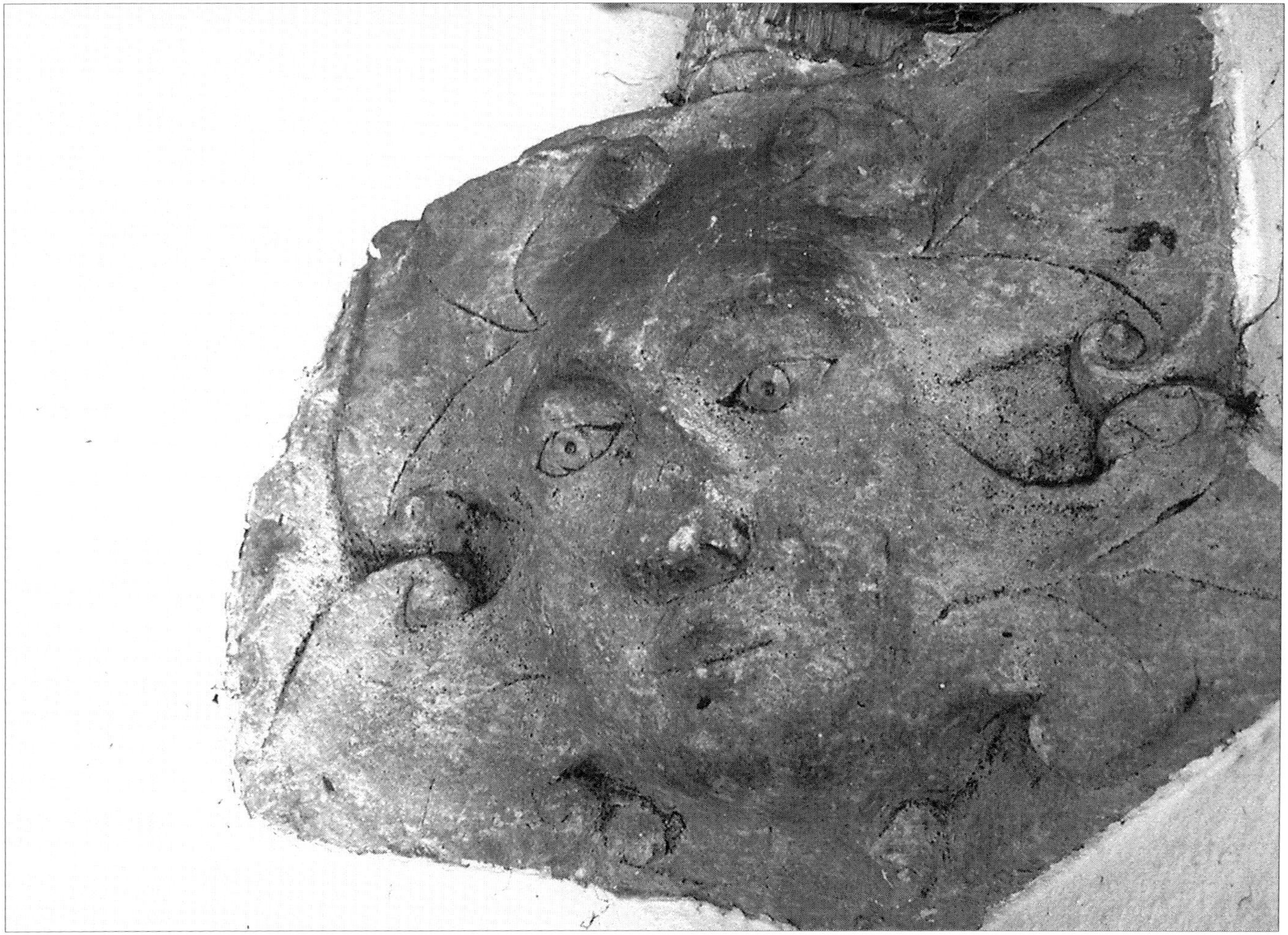

FIGURE 21: *All Saints Church, Great Braxted*

Figure 22: *St Martin's Church, Colchester*

On first sighting the largest pig sitting next to the lion mask may appear to be a green pig, but is in fact a Green Man. His face appears firmly human, but has pig-like features. One has only to look at the other green pig in the chimera to see the contrast. [FIGURES 23, 24 & 25]

This kind of imagery would be easily read by the medieval onlooker for whom this kind of church etiquette was a part of everyday life. Monkeys were exotic creatures and knowledge of them came from a bestiary; a book about beasts and animal-lore. It was made available to everyone, illiterate and educated alike. It symbolised certain animals with supernatural powers and equated them with Christian values. Monkeys represented the devil or his demons.

Similarly St John the Baptist Church in Finchingfield has a wooden tongue-poking Green Man situated over the central arch. Some might debate that he is actually a green lion but I think his face counts as human. [FIGURES 26 & 27]

An intricate 14th century carving of a Green Man features on a tomb spandrel in the church of St John the Evangelist in the village of Little Leighs. He is well hidden amongst other elaborate carvings. [FIGURE 28]

Another splendid face in the opposite spandrel is the tongue poking lion head with branches coming from his mouth which trails off into flowers. [FIGURE 29]

The tomb lying beneath consists of a life-sized oak effigy of a priest in mass vestments. Given that this is the only wooden effigy of a priest known in England, I think we can safely dispel any theory which suggests that the Green Man was a secret pagan flourish of masons. Nor is he a symbol of spring and fertility, as so popularly believed. Clearly the Green Man was part of the church's symbolic language. The effigy in question was purposely made of wood so that it would be easy to move to make a place for the Easter sepulchre. [FIGURE 30]

A beautifully intricate early 16th century Green Man in St Catherine's Church, Gosfield is found on a screen behind the choir stalls. Leaves are draped on his fore-head. The body of the female figure on the right curls round to terminate in a leaf. [FIGURE 31]

It's fairly unusual for a 16th century Green Man to be found in a church, as at this point in the Green Man's history, he was moving outside churches and became more ornamental. I was told by the church warden here that it is believed that this screen was moved to

FIGURE 23: *St Michael's Chruch, Great Sampford*

Figure 24: *St Michael's Chruch, Great Sampford*

FIGURE 25: *St Michael's Chruch, Great Sampford*

FIGURE 26: *St John the Baptist's Church, Finchingfield*

FIGURE 27: *St John the Baptist's Church, Finchingfield*

FIGURE 28: *St John the Evangelist's Church, Little Leighs*

Figure 29: *St John the Evangelist's Church, Little Leighs*

Figure 30: *St John the Evangelist's Church, Little Leighs*

Figure 31: *St Catherine's Church, Gosfield*

the church from Gosfield Hall which was built about 1530 which had a huge amount of panelling,

The Green Man was constantly changing and developing. The Castle Museum in Colchester has a 16th century bearded Green Man with vine leaves sprouting from his mouth. He used to grace the corner post of a house that once stood in the High Street. It is evident that the Green Man has undergone a transformation. He is very ornamental and is found on a domestic building due to the influence of the Reformation and the Renaissance. [FIGURE 32]

The Green Man reappeared in the 17th century in memorials and the elaborate title pages of early printed books. In the 18th century he emerged on Scottish Gravestones which is curious given the Presbyterian aversion to the old faith and "Popish images". But again it is possible that the Green Man was not seen to be linked with Catholic ritual otherwise it would not have been allowed. Another layer of meaning was given to this symbol. The idea that we come from the earth and one day must return to it: "ashes to ashes, dust to dust" comes to mind. The Green Man's meaning now symbolised resurrection.

Similarly Puritans and Presbyterians who settled in

FIGURE 32: *Castle Museum, Colchester*

America and forbade the depiction of the human face also have the Green Man appearing on their gravestones. They are also to be found on "four sides of a foot-high tomb in Elora, Ontario, Canada, an area that was populated by Scottish settlers".

In the Victorian era the Green Man's meaning changes once again as he emerged with profusion on public buildings probably due to their fascination with the Gothic. But he was considered merely as an attractive motif purely for street decoration.

The 13th century Cressing Temple Barns in Braintree (built for the Knights Templar) has four decorative Victorian Green Men at the fount in the form of gargoyle-like spouts in the centre of the lovely walled garden. [FIGURE 33]

On the wall of the Templar Café (next to the gift shop) there is a display of Green Men donated by the Mid Essex Guild of Weavers, Spinners and Dyers in April 2011. This particular Green Man was woven by Mrs Doreen Hawkins and is a variation on the theme – a wonderfully creative Green Man that winks at us playfully. [FIGURE 34]

At SS Mary and Lawrence Church in Great Waltham there are splendid Victorian dragons on the lych gate. But whether they count as 'green' is debatable as the foliate trail appears to stem from behind him rather than directly from his mouth, so this one may be down to personal interpretation. [FIGURE 35 & 36]

Although Victorians restored medieval Green Men in churches, it is unusual that a Victorian caste of a Green Man dwells on the outside west wall of the 12th century church, St Nicholas, in South Ockendon. He appears to serve the same purpose as a gargoyle; he has a pipe running through him, but has foliage coming from his mouth and on top of his head. One can only guess that he was replacing a predecessor who may have served as a protective function to ward off evil spirits. [FIGURE 37]

St Mary the Virgin Church in Great Dunmow houses a 20th century Green Man which replaces his medieval ancestor and like the South Ockendon Green Man has the task of being a gargoyle as he has a pipe running through him also. [FIGURE 38]

Some may think the clergy were simply following established traditions, unaware of the symbolic or historical significance of the Green Man, but I think that is highly questionable. It is much more likely that

Figure 33: *Cressing Temple Barns, Braintree*

Figure 34: *Templar Café, Cressing Temple Barns, Braintree*

FIGURE 35: *SS Mary and Lawrence's Church, Great Waltham*

Figure 36: *SS Mary and Lawrence's Church, Great Waltham*

Figure 37: *St Nicholas' Church, South Ockendon*

FIGURE 38: *St Mary the Virgin's Church, Great Dunmow*

the Green Man's popularity is owed to what is commonly termed the "12th century renaissance movement" in which Catholics enthusiastically drew upon ancient images and ideas to reinforce the Church's teachings.

So it appears that the Green Man may well have been used in this way. The concept of *viriditas*, "the greening of the soul" by the sacred life force of God's spirit was key to the visionary thinking of 12th-century Benedictine, Hildegarde of Bingen, as was God breathing viriditas into Adam and Eve to give them life.

However there are still unknown meanings, such as tongue-poking Green Men which became widespread although the meaning is ambiguous; it could have sexual connotations, express revulsion or was possibly a way of warding off evil.

The church of St Mary the Virgin in Henham, has an ornate tongue-poking late 15th century Green Man which hides itself on the rood screen gate in amongst a multitude of decorative foliage. [FIGURE 39]

In Clavering SS Mary and Clement Church have a 12th century wooden tongue-poking Green Man who is roof beam boss in the south porch. [FIGURE 40]

In the lovely church of St Mary the Virgin in the village of Little Dunmow, a roguish tongue-poking 14th century Green Man is hidden away in a panel below the sill of a window. [FIGURE 41]

The church of St Mary at Antioch in Margaretting, Essex, houses a tongue-poking Green Man with a large oak leaf coming out each side of his mouth. It may be possible to arrange with a church warden for the house next door to give you a key to the church. [FIGURE 42]

A colourful tongue-poking Green Man has managed to survive in the belfry at the west end of All Saints Church in Stock. Inside a stairs which resembles a rickety old ladder leads you up to a late 15th century Green Man with a very human rounded face with a wreath of colourful leaves. It is the only belfry in Essex to have a cruciform plan (in the shape of a cross.) It is a separate structure and only joined to the rest of the church by the eastern arm of the cross. [Figures 43 & 44]

These menacing faces may be the Church's representation of the devil incarnate or sinful flesh.

FIGURE 39: *St Mary the Virgin's Church, Henham*

Figure 40: *SS Mary and Clement's Church, Clavering*

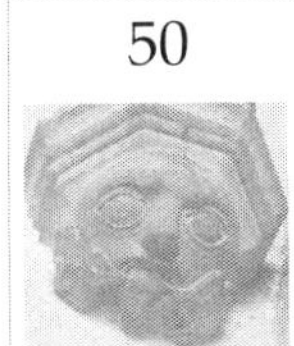

Figure 41: *St Mary the Virgin's Church, Little Dunmow*

FIGURE 42: *St Mary at Antioch's Church, Margaretting*

FIGURE 43: *All Saints' Church, Stock*

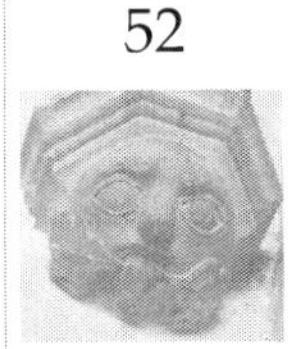

Figure 44: *All Saints' Church, Stock*

Possibly his origins may be attributable to what lurked in the forest; a tree demon or spirit. But we cannot be sure as these captivating carvings are shrouded in 'the unknown'. Amazingly, no written records exist to direct us about his meaning. But what we do know is that many religions and cultures throughout the centuries have given the Green Man different meanings which suited their own particular needs.

In the medieval May Day festival a man covered all over in leaves would predominate over the activities. This has been frequently confused with the Green Man. Contrary to popular belief he did not represent the coming of spring. He was a "Wild Man" personifying sin and the friction between good and evil; an unrelated myth.

Although the term *Green Man is relatively modern* as it was invented in the 20th century, it has sometimes led to confusion as this term was sometimes used in earlier centuries to describe another image which we know as *Woodwose, Woodhouse* or *Wildman* of the woods. The name Woodwose comes from the Old English word *wudu meaning woodland being*. The Middle English word wood which was actually *written as wod* means mad or furious which is where the other alliterative meaning *wild* comes in.

This is one of the very few carvings of a 15th century Wild Man typically carrying a club. It is taken from a spire on St John the Baptist and St Laurence Church in the picturesque town of Thaxted. [FIGURE 45]

But the real McCoy is found hidden at the back of the altar. You have to look carefully at this photo to register the face of this Green Man as he blends in with his surroundings. [FIGURE 46]

In the 1800s a quite separate version of the medieval May Day festival was revived. A "Jack-in-the-Green", enclosed in a pyramidal framework of wickerwork decorated with foliage headed a procession of workers.

At this point we must turn to Lady Raglan, perpetrator of the broad label "Green Man" which she gave to the foliated head found in churches. She believed his history belonged to the Jack-in-the-Green and as much as we would love to join her in believing that the Jack-in-the-Green is a deeply rooted pagan god of our past; he is actually a late 18th century invention. The Jack-in-the-Green is represented as an ancient fertility symbol personifying

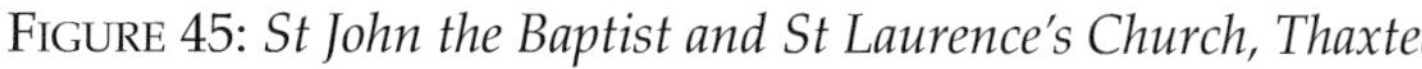

FIGURE 45: *St John the Baptist and St Laurence's Church, Thaxted*

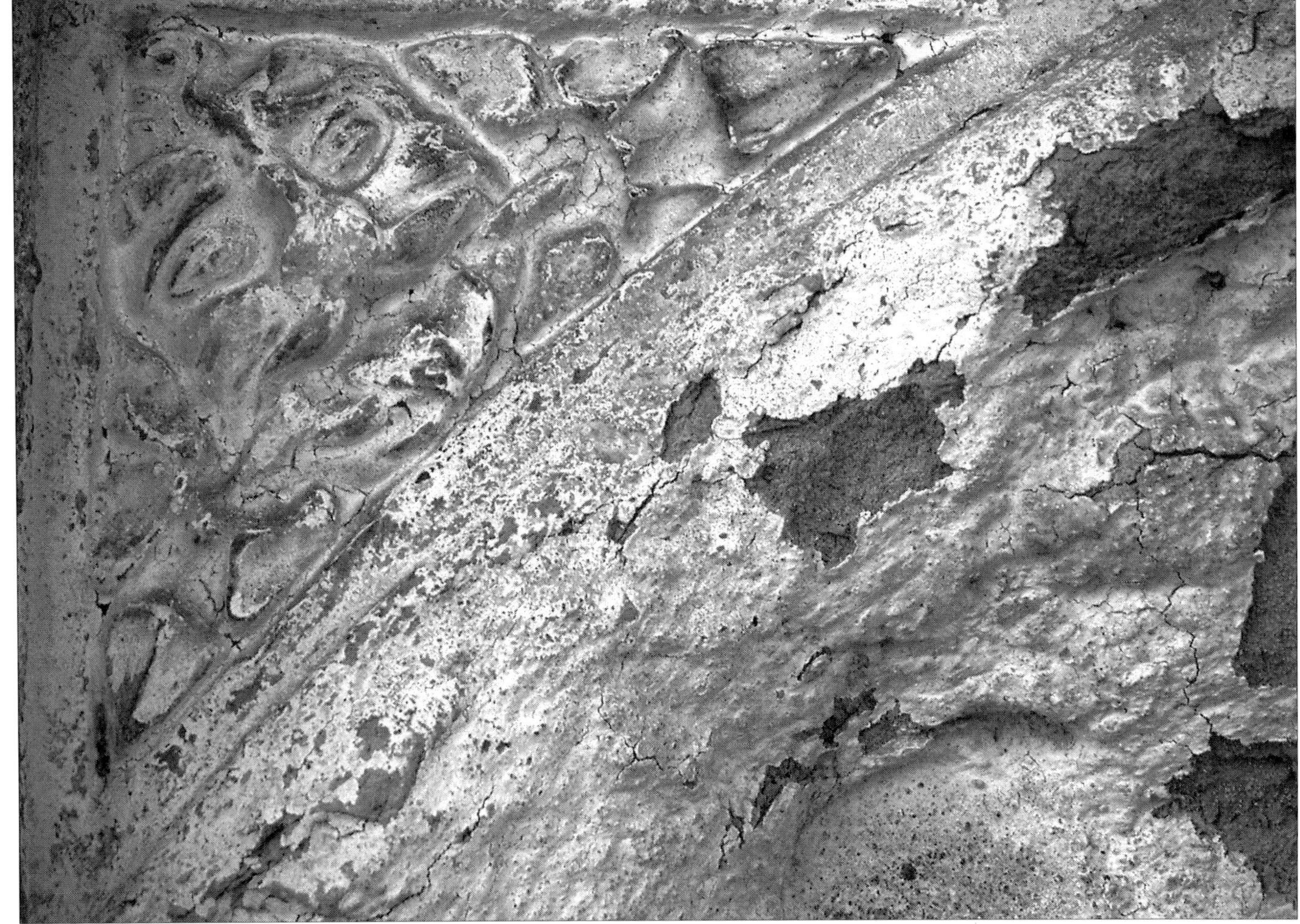

Figure 46: *St John the Baptist and St Laurence's Church, Thaxted*

springtime and the reawakening of nature; a somewhat romantic deviation with a lack of any substantial evidence. It is a seductive theory and perhaps that is why it is so readily accepted.

These suppositions were reaffirmed in 1949 by an article which claimed that a major influence coincided with the medieval era: *Gawain and the Green Knight* – a magical tale about a green knight on a green horse who is beheaded only to pick up his head and ride off representing the "death" of vegetation in the Autumn, "rebirth" in the midwinter and "growth" again in the spring.

This was further reinforced by John Spier's opinion that the Green Man was a descendant of the vegetation or nature god whose death and resurrection mythologises the annual death and rebirth of nature. This caught on as a popular view, so much so, that the Green Man has also been attributed to the song, *John Barleycorn* (The Corn or Barley God) who was resurrected after death in the shape of a tree growing out of his head; Jack-in-the-Green, Green George, the character Puck in Shakespeare's *Midsummer Night's Dream* and even Robin Hood.

In reality few Green Men have tranquil expressions related to the first stirrings of spring. Instead they seem roguish, tormented, lost, and even evil. Many appear disguised and a casual eye might dismiss them as decorative foliage as this flexible icon was frequently used as a space-filler.

But not all Green Men are hidden or austere and consequently not all green men have the same meaning. However many prominent Green Men were destroyed along with other Catholic imagery during the reformation to make way for the new Protestant religion.

Throughout England there are many pubs called the "Green Man" which usually have a sign outside of a man clad in green possibly associated with Robin Hood or a forester figure. But it is extremely unlikely to be a link with the medieval Green Man found in churches. Ironically in the 1980's television series, *Robin of Sherwood*, Robin Hood was referred to as son of Herne, the Horned God concerned with the balance of nature.

A few of these pub signs have been replaced with an ancient foliated head which is fast becoming a fashionable trend. Examples are The Green Man pub in the village of Toot Hill. Obviously the artist has

made a connection between the Green Man and the druidic site of Stonehenge. There is also a foliated Green Man pub sign at Great Waltham and Herongate. [FIGURES 47, 48 & 49]

If we could travel back in time, the medieval Church would bear no relation to the grey dusty churches we see today. Instead, painted pupils of gold-skinned Green Men would bring them alive and we'd be met with with an earthly splendour of gargoyles and animal faces ablaze with colour and pungent with incense.

The Green Man is known variously to us as the Green Man, Jack-in-the-Green, May King, Lord of the Hunt and Green George. It is with caution we should interpret foliate heads of different periods to avoid a hotchpotch of myths from other epochs and terrains. Nobody really knows who he is which merely adds to his charm.

The Green Man is a compelling universal symbol found throughout the world. He resonates with nature and spirituality renewing the many layers of meaning we have chosen to give him throughout the ages. So I am very glad to have found him on my own doorstep flourishing contentedly in the many medieval churches of Essex.

End Note

On page 39 a quotation about Scottish settlers is made. This is a reference to Betty Willsher's article: *The Green Man as an emblem on Scottish Tombstones*. (P.61) published in *Markers: the Association for Gravestone Studies Journal IX* (1992).

The green cat picture in Castle Hedingham was kindly provided by Ruth Wylie.

FIGURE 47: *The Green Man, Toot Hill*

FIGURE 48: *The Green Man, Great Waltham*

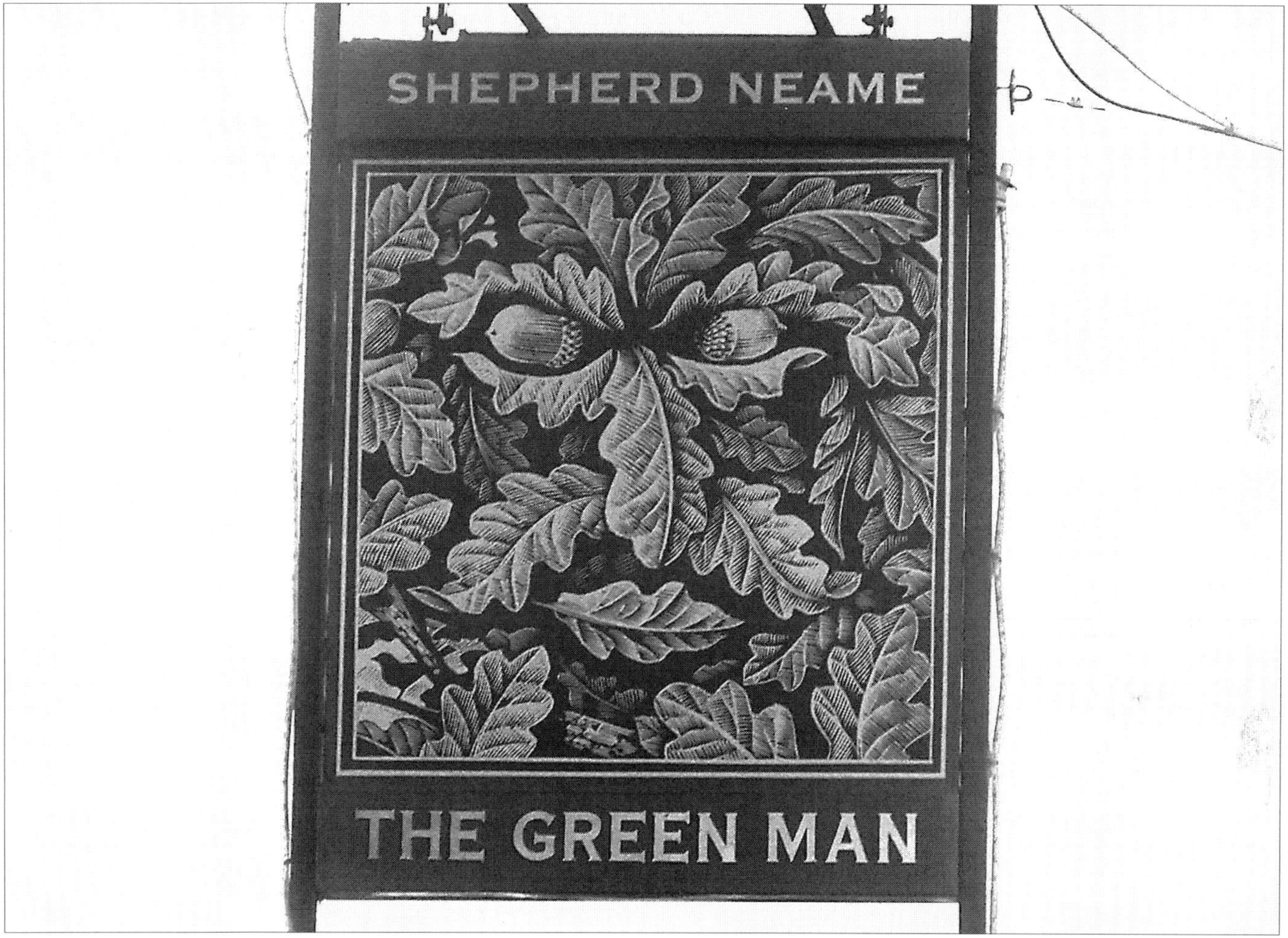

FIGURE 49: *The Green Man, Herongate*

Glossary

CAPITAL	Decorative cap or crown that divides a column or pier
CHANCEL	the front part of the church form where the service is conducted
CORBEL	A block of stone bonded into a wall, supporting the end of a beam
GROTESQUE	Decoration which either interweaves human and animal form with vegetation, or consists of a distorted face
LYCH GATE	A place that provided shelter and a resting place for coffin bearers on the way to church
MISERICORD	Shelf on a carved bracket on the underside of a hinged choir stall seat
NAVE	The main body of the church, where the congregation sits
POPPYHEAD	Decorative ornament on the ends of a church pew or choir-stall.
ROOF BOSS	Carving found on ceilings used to conceal breaks in vault work
SCREEN	A screen dividing the chancel and the nave
SEPULCHRE	An arched recess generally in the north wall of the chancel in which from Good Friday to Easter day were deposited the crucifix and sacred elements in commemoration of Christ's entombment and resurrection
SOUTH DOOR	This is the door the congregation entered through
SPANDREL	The area between two arches
STOUP	A container for holy water

Covers:

Front: All Saints, Stock; *large picture. Left to right:* St Mary of Antioch, Margaretting; All Saints, Maldon; St Nicholas, South Ockendon; St John the Baptist, Finchingfield.

Back: *Left to right:* St Catherine, Gosfield; St Martin, Colchester; St Michael, Great Sampford; Colchester.